The Dog Nobody Wanted

by

Margaret Seiders-Metz

PITTSBURGH, PENNSYLVANIA 15222

The contents of this work including, but not limited to, the accuracy of events, people, and places depicted; opinions expressed; permission to use previously published materials included; and any advice given or actions advocated are solely the responsibility of the author, who assumes all liability for said work and indemnifies the publisher against any claims stemming from publication of the work.

All Rights Reserved
Copyright © 2005 by Margaret Seiders-Metz
No part of this book may be reproduced or transmitted in any form or by any means, electronic or mechanical, including photocopying, recording, or by any information storage and retrieval system without permission in writing from the author.

ISBN # 0-8059-9716-4
Printed in the United States of America

First Printing

For additional information or to order additional books,
please write:
RoseDog Publishing
701 Smithfield Street
Pittsburgh, Pennsylvania 15222
U.S.A.
1-800-834-1803
Or visit our web site and on-line bookstore at
www.rosedogbookstore.com

This book is dedicated to all the loving people that have adopted those unwanted pets and gave them the love and care that they needed. God Bless You All!

Acknowledgments

Thanks goes to Mike Giometti and the staff at the Prairie Trails Public Library, who have gone out of their way to help me get information I needed to publish this book. I would like to thank my husband Robert Metz for having the patience for putting up with my absence while I worked on my manuscript.
    I Love You!

Queenie

It was a dark, cold, rainy night that a half starved, soaked Belgium Shepherd mix named Queenie went into labor. She gave birth to seven mixed breed puppies under a cold, dirty porch. Queenie had a very rough time but did the best she could under the circumstances. She cleaned off the puppies and fed them even though she was very weak herself.

You could see her ribs through her mangled hair on her body. She snuggled her puppies close to her body to keep them warm since it was very cold outside. It was still raining hard and the rain started to seep in where they were all laying. So Queenie picked each puppy in her mouth and carried them one by one to a dryer spot in an old shed nearby that had the door ajar.

It wasn't a nice warm home like she was raised in but it was dry and safe for the time being. Queenie got all her puppies comfortable and started to feed them the best she could since it was days she had eaten anything herself. She cleaned herself up and fell asleep snuggling her body around all the puppies to keep them warm and safe. While the puppies slept, she gently slipped out of the shed to try to find something to eat for herself.

Queenie needed her strength now that she had a new family to take care of. Today was her lucky day. It was garbage day and there were cans set outside by the houses in the neighborhood for the waste management to pick up. As Queenie went from can to can it wasn't looking good since the cans had heavy covers on top of them and she couldn't lift them off.

She finally spotted an open can without a cover at the end of the block. It was filled with plastic garbage bags loaded with trash. Some crows had ripped open the bags and you could see the waste inside. Queenie jumped up to see what she could salvage to eat but she had to watch what she ate so the puppies wouldn't get sick since they were feeding off her.

She found and ate some stale slices of bread, a half eaten hamburger and soggy french fries. To her this was a meal fit for a king because she hadn't eaten for days. She washed it all down with the rainwater near a curb. Now she felt a little better that her stomach had some food in it.

Queenie hurried back to her puppies who were busy trying to find their mama for feeding time. She laid down and all seven of them began to enjoy their breakfast. While they were eating Queenie had a chance to really check them out since it was light outside now.

The light glared through the broken window and the door that was ajar. They were so pretty and very tiny and each one was different. Queenie started licking the first born who was white with tan

Freckles, Lady, Missy, Diamond, Shannon, Stormy, and Teezer

and black spots and was a female. Her name will be Lady. The second pup was white and dark brown, a female also and I'll call her Missy. A third pup was black with a white spot on her chest that looked like a diamond so I'll call her Diamond and she was a female too.

The fourth was another female, sort of yellowish in color. I'll call her Shannon. The fifth pup was like a black and white fuzzball and was also female. She looked like she would tease so I'll call her Teezer. The sixth puppy was another female and she looked like me when I was a puppy. Black and reddish brown, and since she was born in a storm, I'll call her Stormy. The seventh and last puppy was the only male and looked like his daddy, a mix of black, brown and white and I'll call him Freckles.

The puppies were a mixture of every breed, what you would call a Heinz 57. But I didn't care I loved them all. No matter what or who they looked like. They were all mine. Lady could pass for an Australian Shepherd mix. Missy looked like a Brittany Spaniel. Diamond could pass for a Sheltie. Teezer looked like a Shih-Tzu and Maltese mix. Shannon with her yellowish coloring passed for a Lab. Stormy looked just like me a Shepherd mix. And Freckles was like his daddy, a mutt, a mixture of every breed. They were all lovable, chubby and cute. They looked like they were healthy and were hungry all the time. None of them wanted to play yet just eat and sleep and eat some more. I wish their daddy was here to see them and help me out. I would feel better that there was someone with them when I had to leave them alone so I could find food to eat for myself to keep me healthy for them.

Things would of been different if I didn't run away from my good home that was surrounded with love. I use to live in a nice warm, clean house with a big yard and nice people who took good care of me. But when I saw Rinty, he just stole my heart away and I followed him until I got lost and couldn't find my way back since I never was out of the yard except on a leash with one of my owners. I miss playing with the kids Marcy, Mike and Marie. They sure would enjoy playing with my puppies. I sure screwed up good.

The puppies would of had a nice home to live in, not a damp, cold shed. But then if I didn't run away with Rinty I never would of had these precious puppies. The last day I remember running along the railroad tracks with Rinty as happy as we could be, until this mean man started to chase us and hit Rinty in the head with a big club.

I heard the smack as it hit Rinty's head and he fell down. I kept on running as fast as I could to get away and when I stopped and looked back to see if Rinty was behind me, I didn't see him anywhere in sight. I waited behind an old warehouse for him to catch up with me but it never happened. I started to back track to see where Rinty was. All I could see was his wretched body laying in a pool of blood that was streaming from his head where that man hit him with the club. He wasn't moving at all.

Deep down I knew what had happened to him but I just didn't want to believe it. He was gone and now I was alone. Rinty would of been a good daddy to the pups and he sure would of been proud of them. He probably would of spoiled Freckles because he looked just like him.

It's not easy taking care of seven puppies, especially when I'm not in good health. I felt guilty that the pups didn't have a better place to stay. They are eating more and more and I have to be sure I have enough of milk for all of them. And I have to find good food for myself so I can stay healthy and strong and take good care of them.

I will have to find a nice warm place for us to stay that will be safe for all of us. I have to consider it's not just me alone anymore but all eight of us. And I want all my puppies to be healthy, happy and be lovable. And I aim to be a good mommy to them and protect them.

Just like a child, my puppies need proper nourishment to sustain an active, exuberant life style during their vital growth period. Right now they expend a lot of energy and require a lot of rest. I have to feed them often as poor nutrition can lead to a sick puppy. I have enough of milk for my puppies now but soon they will need all the essential vitamins and minerals in their little bodies.

They will need calcium for strong bones and teeth for development. The puppies will be looking for food to eat with the milk from me. They will have to get check ups and shots to keep them healthy, like I got when I lived with my owners.

They sure are growing fast, and I noticed all the puppies are getting chubbier except for Freckles. It seems all he wants to do is sleep. He even falls asleep while he is feeding and I have to keep waking him up to eat. It looks like he is losing weight instead of putting pounds on. When it was feeding time I purposely would push him first to eat so that he could fatten up, but he just wanted to sleep. He never whined like the other puppies, he would just lay their very quietly and sleep. Even nudging him didn't help.

When the other puppies played, they would even walk on him but he didn't care. Freckles couldn't be bothered, all he wanted to do was sleep, sleep and sleep. I figured I would let him sleep but keep an eye on him at all times to check that he was okay. He was my only male puppy.

I knew something was wrong but what? I would spend equal time playing with the puppies but Freckles wanted no part of it, so I just let him sleep. As all the puppies gathered to eat I noticed Freckles just laid near my body but wasn't eating so I nudged him with my nose and he still didn't move. I tried to move him with my paw and he was limp. I placed my mouth on his and felt no breath and knew that my little Freckles was no longer with us but instead he joined his daddy Rinty up in doggie heaven.

I didn't want to upset the other puppies so I just waited till they finished eating. They all fell asleep after a full stomach. I gently carried my little Freckles in my mouth to the outside. There was a big flower garden and I dug a little grave with my paws for my sweetheart. I kissed Freckles good by and gently laid him in the hole and covered his tiny body with the dirt until you could no longer see him. There were flowers blooming all around him and he was deep enough that no other animal or person would dig him up. I said my prayer for God to watch over him and Rinty and started to head back to my six puppies.

I need help since I'm not feeling well myself and the puppies are going to need food soon. As I laid their surrounded with my family of six I started thinking maybe I can find good homes for them so they can survive and not die like Freckles did. I blamed myself for his death.

If we were living in a house our owners would of taken Freckles to a Animal Hospital and he might still be alive. It's all my fault I'm a rotten mommy. I have to do some thing fast before more of my pups die. I have to protect them not only from sickness but from mean people out there like the man that clubbed their daddy Rinty. It's hard because I can't take them all with me so I will have to do most of my work while they are all sleeping although I do not like to leave them alone so no one will take them or some animal eat them.

I will just have to keep my eyes and ears open to try and find some trusting families that would give them plenty of love and a good warm home to live in. They scatter all over the shed now and it won't be long that I won't be able to keep them together. I have to watch that they don't run away or get in a fight. They might even die of starvation staying with me. They deserve better then me.

Soon the weather will be changing to snow and many blizzards so I will have to work fast to find each puppy a nice home. I promise I will not give them to a home where they would be mistreated or not wanted. I wouldn't forgive myself if they fell into the wrong hands. Time sure flies when your having fun. I can't believe that the puppies are nine weeks old already and getting into any thing and everything. It's hard to keep them together.

I have to find homes sooner then soon like yesterday. There is a park close by where children play on the swings with their parents and other kids maybe I can get lucky. I can take one of the pups there to see if I can find someone to take care of her. Lady would have to be the first because she was the first one born and is the oldest. The puppies were getting noisy and I had to be sure no one could hear them so they wouldn't throw us out of the shed or hurt them. Please God help me to find good homes for all my pups fast.

While the puppies were sound asleep I carried Lady in my mouth gently so as not to hurt her. I walked across to the park and set her down near a park bench. There were some children playing on the swings with their moms. Some were in the sandbox. Two boys were riding their bikes with their dads through the park. I kissed Lady good by and told her to stay there while I went to hide behind some bushes to see if anyone would take her home with them. No one seemed to pay any attention to her at all.

I waited and watched to be sure no harm came to Lady. I saw a man jogging Lady's way. He was wearing a shirt that had Bob on it which must of been his name. He spotted Lady and picked her up. Well, well what have we here? You sure are a cutie. Where did you come from? Are you lost? Lady couldn't stop licking the man's face.

The man just glowed with joy over Lady. He checked all around but saw no one and said I guess I'll have to take you home with me so you don't get run over by a bike or hurt. I will run an ad in the newspaper under found a dog. I'm sure someone will claim such a cute little puppy, and if no one does I'll just keep you for myself. I don't have much money but I don't think you eat that much. I'm alone and so are you so we can make each other happy, okay?

Lady wagged her tail as if she understood what the man had said. Queenie was glad she found this man named Bob to take care of Lady. Now she will have a good home and will be very spoiled since this man was crazy about Lady. They both looked so happy as Lady's tongue was licking Bob's face and her tail was wagging just as fast.

I returned back to the shed to take care of my five other puppies. I already missed Lady, my white, black and tan spotted sweetheart. I hope she will understand why I had to give her up in order for her to survive. She will always be in my heart. I snuggled with my pups and fell fast asleep. When I woke up it was meal time again. These puppies should be eating food now not just milk.

I cleaned each pup off and we played a little. Boy I sure was tired and could use a nap but no way, not with five little trouble makers around just waiting to get into everything. I planned to take Missy, my white and dark brown pup that looked like a Brittany Spaniel and find a good home for her.

After a good nights sleep and the pups' bellies were full and they were sleeping again I carried Missy gently in my mouth and walked to a grade school that was a block away. The children would be coming out to play for recess soon so I will have to hurry and set Missy down near the playground. I told her to stay and I ran around the back of the building where I could watch Missy and not be seen by anyone.

Ring, ring went the school bell as the children began to come out and play for recess. Some headed for the swings while others, jumped rope. Two girls were playing in the sand box and some boys were playing ball. Three boys were chasing some of the girls and there were four boys hanging upside down on the monkey bars. A small boy named Brian saw Missy while hanging upside down and almost fell off the monkey bars. He landed on his butt and Missy came running towards him.

When she reached him she started licking his face like crazy and it caused Brian to giggle out loud. Brian picked up Missy and yelled I found a puppy and it's mine. She likes me see, she can't stop licking me. By now there were many children that gathered around to pet Missy. Soon one of the teachers approached Brian to see what all the big commotion was all about, She picked up the puppy and took Brian by the hand and they all went to see the principle.

Brian kept on crying and yelling, it's my puppy, I found her. The principle called Brian's parents and told them to please come down to the school because they could not stop Brian from crying and yelling. Brian held on to the puppy until his parents came. His mother named Joanne and his dad Mike with his sister Chrissy walked up to Brian to see what was the matter. Brian said mommy can I keep her she likes me? Can I mom please?

One look at Missy and Brian's mom fell in love with her. Chrissy wanted to hold the puppy and when she did the puppy started licking her face too. Mike took the puppy from her and you could tell the pup was very happy from the way it's tail was wagging. It was wagging so fast it was like a fan turned on full force. The four of them left the school with the puppy so they wouldn't disrupt the class anymore.

They agreed to keep the puppy unless someone claims her. And if no one does they will keep her since they all fell in love with her. Queenie saw how happy she was and how happy they were to have her so she felt relieved that she found someone to love her and take good care of her, better then she could right now. Freckles had a good home in heaven with his daddy and Lady was with that nice man Bob and now Missy has a loving family to take care of her so that leaves four more puppies to find homes for.

Queenie went back to the shed where her puppies were waiting to be fed by her. After meal time and play time was over Queenie fell sound asleep thinking if she was doing the right thing by giving her puppies away but what else was she supposed to do? She now would have to choose puppy number three and try to find a good home for her. One where she would be loved and wanted.

Diamond was selected to be the next lucky pup. She was the puppy that looked like a Sheltie with a white diamond shape on her chest. After Queenie fed her puppies and they fell sound asleep, she sneaked out of the shed carrying Diamond gently with her mouth. There was this family not to far away that had two children who wanted a puppy real bad but couldn't afford to buy one right now.

They seemed like a nice family, a dad named Ron and a mom called Marie. They had a boy named Nicky and a girl Marissa. They loved dogs so I knew they would be good to Diamond. But how in the world do I get Diamond in there? I decided to sit Diamond right in front of their door and jumped up to ring their doorbell. I ran real fast across the street to hide in the bushes and watch to see what would happen when they came to answer the door.

The boy opened the front door and saw no one but his sister who is quite small and was standing next to him saw this cute little puppy by her feet. She picked the pup up. Nick and Marissa were fighting over who would carry the puppy in the house. They were both yelling. Mom! Mom! Look at what we found by the door, a cute little puppy. They both were so excited that they forgot to shut the front door so I got to see and hear what was going on in their house. Their mom took the pup from Nicky's arms and asked them where the puppy came from? Marissa ran to her dad and told him the puppy came to live with her. Come see daddy, come on!

The mom and dad said the puppy must be lost. She sure is cute and oh so soft. Marissa kept saying my doggie and kept kissing her. Both parents agreed that if no one claims the puppy then Nick and Marissa can keep her. The dad shut the front door but you could still hear all the excitement going on in their house. I found another happy home for my puppy that had kids to play with. I know that Diamond will love it here and be very happy.

The next lucky puppy to find a good home for would be Shannon the one that looked like a yellow Labrador. I headed back to the shed where my decreasing family was waiting for me to return. My heart ached to be giving my little darlings away but there was no sense in lying to myself that as a good mother I had to do what was best for all of them. And the best thing I could do was to find. each puppy a good loveable home.

I had to be careful because I wanted people who will treat my puppies right, maybe even spoil them rotten. I know God will watch over them and protect them. I spent some time playing with the remaining pups. I fed them and licked them clean and off to la la land we all went. We all cuddled close to one another to keep warm. As I laid there surrounding my puppies, I really missed Freckles, Lady, Missy and Diamond but I know they will forgive me because now they have a warm home and nice people who will take good care of them.

The next morning it turned extremely cold and was raining pretty hard. Even though my puppies weren't getting wet, they were shivering from the cold and dampness. I tried to snuggle them closer to my body to keep them all warmer but they were still shaking from the cold. I saw a dark shadow of a man come into the shed and he heard the pups whining. I tried to keep them quiet but it just didn't work.

The tall man came over to where we were all laying. He looked at us and said this is no place to be on a cold stormy day with a family. He very gently picked up the three puppies and held them in his folded arms and called to me to follow him. He took all of us into his warm and cozy house. His wife brought in a crate and lined it with a blanket and set each pup inside the crate.

They moved the crate in front of the fireplace to keep us warm. The man motioned to me to lay down by the fireplace near the pups. It sure felt nice and warm not like the cold shed. He looked like a farmer wearing bibbed-overalls. His wife was baking bread and the whole house sure did smell good. She was cooking some kind of beef stew on the stove which smelled even better.

She was an elderly woman with a very kind face. She ripped some of the bread into tiny pieces and poured some fresh milk over it and gave it to the puppies to eat. They sure enjoyed it and licked the bowl clean. Then in another bowl she ripped some more of the bread into bigger pieces and poured some of the stew over it and set it down in front of me to eat.

I gobbled it down so fast and the lady told me to slow down there was plenty more. I not only licked the bowl clean but all her fingers too. I couldn't remember when was the last time I had a good meal or even when I ate last. I've been living out of garbage cans and dumpsters or scraps from wherever I found them. She put some more food into my bowl and dipped her fingers into the gravy and let the puppies lick her fingers clean. It was like I died and went to heaven. I walked over to where she was siting and gave her a big lick on her face to tell her thank you and she giggled.

The farmer let me outside to relieve myself and he waited by the door till I was ready to come back in. When I returned to the fireplace the woman was freshening the blanket in the crate for the puppies. After she put them all back into the crate I crawled in and cuddled the pups near me. With the heat from the fireplace and our bellies full, we all fell fast asleep. I was so grateful that this man found us because if he didn't maybe I would of lost my three puppies from the cold.

The farmer and his wife discussed about what to do with the pups and me. They couldn't keep all of us so they decided to run an ad in the newspaper. Puppies free to good home, no papers and not house broken. Call any time and left their phone number. Well it wasn't long after the ad ran that a family called to come and see the pups. It was a woman named Marcia and her husband John with three boys. I heard her call them Steven, Daniel and Kevin.

They weren't interested in me because I was to old and shaggy looking but they did check out all three of the pups and decided to take Shannon, the one that looked like a yellowish Labrador. They all took turns holding her. And when Kevin held her she wouldn't stop licking his face until Daniel took the pup from him. Then the boy called Steven took the pup for awhile. They all agreed this was the puppy they wanted even though the others were cute too.

Well thanks to the farmer and his wife, another of my puppies found a good home with caring owners and kids to play with. That leaves only two more puppies that need a home. I still feel very weak and sluggish. I hope I'm not sick because I don't want my puppies to get sick from me. I'll probably feel better tomorrow. Lets see who is next to find a good home and owner for Little Teezer. She is so cute that I shouldn't have any trouble finding someone to love her and take good care of her.

She is just a big ball of black and white fuzz and has the biggest dark brown eyes that can melt your heart away. A week passed and no one has come to inquire about the free puppies. I can enjoy them a little longer. I felt very sick and couldn't stop shaking all over but felt very hot. The farmer's wife wrapped me in a blanket and placed me by the fireplace but I was still shivering.

The farmer told his wife he better take me to see the veterinarian to have me checked over and maybe he could give me medicine to help me out. The puppies stayed home in the crate while the farmer picked me up still wrapped in the warm blanket. He laid me in the back of his truck. I was so weak that I couldn't stand up even if I wanted to. I would never forgive myself if my puppies got sick from me. I will just have to keep away from them until I'm better. I wouldn't hurt my little darlings in any way I love them to much.

When we arrived at the Veterinary Hospital, the nurse took me and laid me on a cold steel table, and unwrapped the blanket around me. The doctor came in and took my temperature and it was high. He listened to my chest and told the farmer I had Pneumonia. Doctor Hites gave me a shot and gave the farmer medication to give me and said to keep me warm and away from the pups. He told him to bring me back in a week unless I got worst.

It seemed like it took forever to get home. I was so very tired and hot. The farmer had to carry me in the house where he placed me in front of the fireplace and covered me with the blanket. The farmer's wife sat down on the floor next to me and kept petting my head. Every time I would move the blanket off of me because I was so hot, she would just cover me up again. The puppies were on the far side of the fireplace.

I was to weak to eat or drink. They would pour water in their hands for me to drink but my head was to heavy to lift so the wife would just wet my mouth and nose. All I wanted to do was sleep just like Freckles did. The farmer's wife fed the pups since I couldn't go near them. I felt so bad. What kind of mommy was I that I couldn't feed my own pups? The farmer gave me some medicine in my mouth and I fell into a deep sleep.

I dreamed I was playing with all my puppies in the warm sun in a field filled with flowers galore. We were all so happy running around chasing each other.

The next morning the farmer's wife came over to check on Queenie. She was laying the same way from last night. She was very still and the farmer's wife taught Queenie was still sleeping, but she noticed that the dog wasn't breathing. She called for her husband and he held his hand on Queenie's chest but felt no movement at all. He picked her up in the blanket and they both rushed her to the doctor.

When they got to the clinic the farmer carried Queenie and she was so limp and heavy. Doctor Hites asked them to step out into the waiting room while he examined Queenie. In a short time the doctor came out and walked over to the farmer and his wife and said I'm sorry but she suffered a stroke during the night and with the Pneumonia and high fever she just didn't survive.

She won't be suffering anymore now she is in God's hands. The farmer's eyes got very teary as his wife wiped away her teardrops. The doctor said don't blame yourselves because you both did everything you could. I wish I could of saved her but I can't perform miracles. The farmer's wife asked what will we do with her two puppies? We tried to find homes for them but still have two left and no one has come to see them recently. Doctor Hites suggested that they bring the two remaining pups into the clinic and maybe he might have better luck finding them a home.

The farmer and his wife left Queenie to be cremated and went back home to get the two puppies to bring them to the clinic. When they arrived back home the farmer left the motor running while his wife went in to get the pups. To her amazement she only found one in the crate, Teezer. The one that looked like a Shih-Tzu. The mixed Shepherd, Stormy was no where in sight. She looked all over and whistled for the other puppy but no luck.

The wife ran out to the truck to tell her husband one of the puppies was missing. The farmer turned off the motor and went inside to check if he could find the pup. He said she couldn't have gone to far, just keep looking. They both searched everywhere. High and low, in and out, under the beds and couches, even out in the shed and barn. But neither one could find her. So they took Teezer only back to the veterinarian. The farmer drove the truck while his wife held fuzzy little Teezer on her lap and they both kept watching the road to see a lost puppy appear.

They took Teezer inside and explained to the doctor that the other puppy was lost. Doctor Hites said not to worry that she would probably turn up when she got hungry. He took Teezer from the farmer's arms and said, she sure is a cutie. I don't think we will have any trouble finding her a good home. The farmer and his wife gave Teezer a kiss good by and left teary eyed to go back home.

It was a very hectic day with Queenie dying and losing one of the pups, and taking the other puppy to the clinic, running back and forth to the Veterinarian, that when night time came both the farmer and his wife were so exhausted that they both fell asleep the minute their heads hit their pillows. They both missed the puppies and Queenie but it was for the best because now they will have good homes and maybe children to play with.

Teezer was very frightened being in a strange place without her mama and sister Stormy. What will happen to me now? Where will I go? Who will feed me and take care of me? Will I die too like my brother Freckles and my daddy Rinty and my Mama? Where did all my other sisters go? A pretty nurse came in, unlocked the door to my cage and picked me up. She took me to an examining room and put me on a long table.

The doctor was going to give me what they call a check up. Doctor Hites was a very gentle man and tried to make me feel at home. He weighed me, checked my teeth, eyes, ears, felt all over to check my bones and even checked the condition of my coat. So far this wasn't to bad. I sure was getting a lot of attention. Then I saw him take a long needle and stuck it in my paw and drew out some red stuff called blood. He held the spot where they drew blood to stop it from bleeding. He trimmed my tiny sharp nails.

Then the doctor did what they call a fecal exam to check if I had any worms which most puppies have. Now he came near me with a long needle and ouch! stuck me with it for Distemper, which is a fatal disease that affects the respiratory and intestinal tracts and my nervous system. I heard the doctor tell the nurse I will still need more shots to protect me against Hepatitis which is a viral disease of the liver.

A shot to protect me from getting Parvovirus, which is dangerous for puppies and can cause dehydrating diarrhea. Leptospirosis can cause me permanent kidney damage which can be spread to humans. Coronavirus is highly contagious intestinal disease that causes vomiting and diarrhea and a puppy or dog can die from it. Rabies is the worst feared disease which is fatal because it attacks the brain and central nervous system.

I never knew so many things could go wrong with me. I hope Freckles didn't die from any of these diseases. I wonder if my sisters got shots to keep them healthy. I sure was glad the farmer and his wife dropped me off here so I could get protection from all these bad things. The doctor checked me for kennel cough and heartworm and now I was given a clean bill of health and was ready to be adopted if anyone would want me. The nurse cleaned me up and put me back in the cage with shredded newspaper on the floor.

The nurse left and came back with some fresh cold water in my bowl. I wasn't the only animal here. There were a lot of cages and some were filled with puppies, dogs, cats, kittens and different kinds of birds with pretty colors. Some held mice, rabbits, turtles and in glass tanks were snakes. They were eating while some were sleeping and some just kept on licking themselves clean or just looking around. It was nice and quiet until someone would come into the room, then it would get very noisy.

It sounded like a mad house with all the different sounds coming from different animals. Barking, whining, purring, meowing, chirping, birds singing, parrots talking. But as soon as the person left it would get so quiet that you could hear a pin drop on the floor. As I laid in my cage, I wondered what ever happened to my sister Stormy who ran away. Is she in a nice warm home with kids to play with? Is she in heaven? I miss her I wonder if she forgot me.

I hope nothing happened to her like what happened to our daddy when he ran away with our mom. Their both up in heaven with Freckles. I wish I could see my sisters, Lady, Missy, Diamond, Shannon and Stormy. I sure do miss them. I hope that all of them are safe and living in good homes. I looked around and down the hall was a puppy in a cage that looked like Stormy but it wasn't her. Even though there were all these other animals here I felt so alone. Don't get me wrong, the animals are nice and welcomed me but I want my own family.

I guess I'm what they call a lonely orphan, no mama, no papa and all my sisters and my brother are gone. I cried so hard that I fell asleep. After a good nights rest I woke up when I heard the nurse coming in with bowls of food for the animals. She opened my cage and slipped in a bowl of puppy food. Boy I sure was hungry and ate it all up washing it down with some water. The other animals didn't pay any attention to anybody they were all busy eating too.

I laid in my cage just thinking that all there was left was just the three of us me, myself and I. Or else I could say we three, my echo, my shadow and me. I'm getting silly now that's because I'm scared. I over heard that if no one adopts you they put you to sleep forever. I pray real hard for some one to adopt me. Maybe I should try to run away but where would I go? Anyway it's not to bad here. I don't have kids to play with but I have a clean cage and warm place to stay and food to eat.

It's more than some puppies have so I should be grateful for what I have. Someday my family will be all together again up in heaven. My mama, daddy, Freckles, my only sick brother, and my five sisters Lady, Missy, Diamond, Shannon, Stormy and me, Teezer. There really is nothing to do here except eat and sleep and potty calls and bark.

The nurse came in to change the shredded paper in my cage and gave me nice fresh paper all over the bottom of my cage.

I fell asleep dreaming about my family. I sure missed that warm body of my mama to snuggle by. I hope she is up in heaven with my daddy and that they are both happy. The door opened and some people came in to look at the animals for adoption. Some sat in the waiting room with their pets for exams or shots. Others were dropped off for grooming or to have surgery.

There was a cute little fellow that was to have her teeth cleaned and one tooth pulled out because it was very loose and the doctor didn't want her to swallow it. There were all different breeds, colors and sizes of animals. A woman with her children came over and looked at me and almost took me home with them until they found out I wasn't house broken.

Instead the woman chose a black Poodle named Inky. I sat and watched other dogs and puppies being handled and put back into their cages. Another woman came in with her daughter and they adopted two of the small dogs Daisy and Peaches. They looked so happy that they finally would have a home. The woman looked like she would spoil them rotten, lucky dogs! An older lady came in to adopt a cat. And she left with an older cat named Niky. She sure loved him and bought some cat food and a bunch of cat toys too. A young boy with his dad bought a white Dove. His name was Nick and he wanted the bird for his magic tricks.

The Dove's name was Lulu. The boy was so happy. The dad bought a big cage and bird food and some toys for Lulu and a mirror to admire herself in. Many people and children taught I was very cute but no one was adopting me, why? What was wrong with me? Again I fell asleep crying that no one would ever adopt me and they would just have to put me asleep. I didn't even eat I was so upset I just fell asleep.

The next morning a young boy came in the clinic crying his eyes out, carrying a puppy in his arms that was hardly moving. The doctor asked what was wrong but the boy was crying and you couldn't understand what he was saying. Doctor Hites took the puppy from him and put him on the examining table. He asked again what had happened and the boy answered that he found the puppy wandering around and he didn't want the puppy to get hit by a car so he picked her up and put her in the basket on his bike.

Stormy and Teezer

But as he was peddling fast the puppy jumped out of the basket and fell down, head first. She didn't move at all. I'm sorry, I didn't mean to hurt her, I was trying to protect her from getting hurt. Will she be okay Doc? Huh? Doctor Hites told the boy that the puppy would have to stay overnight to see that there were no internal injuries or bleeding. As far as he could tell after checking her, that she didn't have any broken bones.

The doctor told the boy to come back tomorrow and we will have her as good as new. The boy kissed the puppy and left. The nurse put the puppy in a clean cage next to mine. She filled her dish with fresh, cool water and spread shredded newspaper on the bottom of her cage. The puppy was moving very slow. It cuddled in the corner of her cage and fell fast asleep.

The longer I stared at the puppy, the more she resembled my lost sister Stormy, who ran away from the farmers house. I tried to talk to her but she was in a sound sleep. Could it be her I wondered? I fell asleep until I heard the nurse come in to take the puppy for some x-rays and a blood test. I heard the puppy squeal when they stuck her in the paw with the needle to draw some blood to be tested. She sure looks like Stormy except she was bigger then me.

Lady and Teezer

But then she would appear bigger because Stormy was like my mom a Shepherd mix while I'm like a Shih-Tzu which is a lot smaller. When the doctor was finished, he brought the puppy back to the cage. The puppy was wide awake now so I tried to find out if she was my sister Stormy. Hi! I said, my name is Teezer, what is yours? How old are you? Where did you come from? What happened to you? Have you any brothers or sisters? I had a million questions to ask. She told me to slow down I'll answer your questions but one at a time please. My head still hurts so take it easy.

My daddy is in doggie heaven, his name was Rinty, and I never knew him because he died before I was born. My mom was very sick and the people where we lived took her away and never brought her back. I got scared and ran away. I had a brother whose name was Freckles and he lives up in heaven too. I even had five sisters Lady, Missy, Diamond, Shannon and hey that's funny because my sister's name was Teezer and she even looked like you too. My mom's name was Queenie and my name is Stormy.

Teezer was overjoyed that now she had found her lost sister Stormy again and yelled across the cages I'm your sister Teezer! I guess I might as well tell you the bad news that our mom is in heaven too. You know that she found good homes for Lady, Missy, Diamond and Shannon, and would of found a home for you and me but she got very sick and died. The farmer and his wife came back from the doctor to take you and me to this place but you were gone and they couldn't find you anywhere. I was so worried about you. Where did you go?

Stormy answered I ran and tried to find my way back but I got lost so I just kept going until this nice boy found me and put me in his basket on his bike. I jumped out and fell down and that's all that I remember. Well Teezer said I'm glad your alright and were together but we both have to hope we get adopted and have a nice warm, loving home. Maybe we will be lucky and someone will adopt the both of us together. But if not at least we can spend our time here together. I sure missed you. Your all I have right now. Mom always said the good Lord would take care of us. So we just have to wait and see what develops for us.

Teezer reminded me that maybe I already have a home with the boy that brought me in here. He told the doctor he would be back to take me out and bring me home with him. We'll see what happens but in the meantime I'm so glad we found each other and I'm sorry I worried you so. The boy did not come back to pick up Stormy. Night time came and he still didn't show up. The nurse came in to turn off the lights and locked the doors since they were closed for the night. Stormy and I talked through our cages in the dark until we both fell asleep.

The next morning the boy came in to the clinic. I could see Stormy's tail wagging like crazy because she taught he was taking her home with him but it didn't turn out that way. The boy told the doctor that his parents wouldn't let him have a puppy because where they lived in an apartment there were no pets allowed. The boy was crying but his parents said no way, no puppy and that's final.

Doctor Hites told the boy he was welcomed to come and visit with the puppy until they found a home for her. Stormy was saddened with the news but adjusted to staying with Teezer until someone adopts one or both of them. It's not to bad here. We have a warm place to stay, fresh clean newspaper changed in our cage, good food, cool water and each other, what more could we ask for except a owner.

The next day when the clinic opened up a nice looking man came in looking for a small size puppy that wouldn't shed. He wanted a female and she didn't have to be house broken. The nurse took him in the room to see the puppies they had. She showed him Stormy but he didn't want a pup that would shed or get big. So she showed him Teezer. She took her out of the cage and let the man hold her. Teezer started licking the man's face. He said she was exactly what he was looking for.

He told the nurse that he already had a Australian shepherd mix puppy and wanted a playmate for her to keep her company while he was at work. She doesn't like to be alone. I love dogs and will give her a good home with a lot of love. The man paid the bill for adopting me and they told him about the shots I received and what other shots I would need. They again warned him that I wasn't housebroken.

As they handed him papers with my name and breed on them I noticed his name was Robert Metz and he lived in a mobile home in Lynwood Illinois. Wow! Now I have my very own owner. I was very happy and yet sad because I just got Stormy back and now we will be apart again. I hope some one adopts her soon so she can be happy too. When we got into his truck, he held me up to look me over and said what a cutie you are, Lady will just love you as much as I do.

He drove to his home with me on his lap. I was to small to see anything out of the windows, so I just looked at him or slept. If I have to say so myself I am a cutie, I look like a ball of black and white hair with two enormous dark brown marble size eyes. When I walk I strut from side to side with my tail up like a feathery plume. My ears are long and black with a little white and I have hair covering my nose. I have grown since I was born but I'm still small. I'm lucky that this man loves me and is gentle and nice to me. Too bad he didn't adopt Stormy too, I just found her and now were apart again.

Back at the animal hospital Stormy was happy for her sister getting adopted but was sad because now she was alone again. She really missed Teezer. Stormy felt like no one would ever adopt her since she looked like a misfit with a broken cartilage in her ear. One ear stood up straight while the other one bent over to say they went that way. I'll just have to wait and be patient for my turn to come and be adopted.

There are a lot of people waiting to adopt dogs and a lot of dogs waiting to be adopted. I'm just afraid that one look at me and no one will adopt me. And if no one adopts me that means they will put me to sleep. That might be okay since I would be with my mama, daddy and Freckles. But what if I didn't go to heaven since I was bad and ran away? Then I would go were the bad dogs go and I don't want to go there. I'll just have to look real pretty and smart and act nice so someone will adopt me. I've seen some dummies and ugly looking dogs that still got adopted so that means there is still hope for me. Look at my mom, she never gave up trying and I'm like her so I won't give up trying. What's meant to be will be. After all things could be worst. I could be starving and cold.

I'm going stir crazy being locked up in this cage. I can't stand it anymore. I'll just have to run away again and find my own owners by myself. I laid there in my lonely cage thinking of how I could escape this place. The Animal Hospital is closed on Sundays and tomorrow is Sunday so I will have to think of something fast. I got so tired of thinking that I fell fast asleep.

Early Sunday morning the doctor's staff came in the room to take the dogs and puppies out of their cages and exercised them in the big back yard while they cleaned and washed down the cages real good and put fresh shredded newspaper in the puppy cages. Now was my chance to escape. With all of them being busy working no one will notice me at all.

I went around the back of the building and started to dig a hole under the cyclone fence that held us in. But my paws are so small it will take forever to dig my way out. But then my body isn't big like some of these dogs that maybe I could squeeze through a small opening. But I have to be very careful so I don't get cut on the sharp bottom of the fence. I glanced around to see if the coast was clear. I could see some dogs were laying in the sun, some were sleeping, one was chasing his tail going in circles. A couple of puppies were running all over the yard. There was a big dog, a Great Dane teasing another dog a German Shepherd.

I noticed a huge Rottweiler heading towards me. What are you doing over here by yourself he asked? I told him I had to get out of here fast. That it meant my sanity. If I stay any longer I'll go nuts being cooped up. He just couldn't believe me that I didn't want to stay here where it was nice and clean, warm and the doctors and nurses took good care of you. Where you got good meals and fresh water everyday it just didn't make sense to leave.

He couldn't understand why I wanted to leave since I had a nice warm place to sleep and a meal everyday. He warned me that I don't know what is out there waiting for me, but I told him I would take my chances. He didn't ask me any more questions just started to help me dig my way out. The size of his paws were so huge that one swift paw hitting the dirt made a hole big enough for me to escape. I thanked him and was on my way. He wished me luck and said I would need it.

I didn't know where I was headed but I had to get far away before they realized I was missing. I'll just follow the roads like in the Wizard of Oz, follow the yellow brick road, except that this road was black tar and some times gravel. I ran and ran till my paws hurt. The Sun was going down and it started to get cold. Even though I have a lot of hair on my body I was shivering. I would run to keep warm and then walk because my paws hurt from running on the gravel.

I was hungry but tried to take my mind off of food since I didn't have any. I quenched my thirst with water along curbs and puddles around lawns that were just sprinkled. It didn't taste like the fresh water in my cage but it will have to do, it's better then nothing. I had no way of knowing where I was going but I kept going till my paws could no longer hold me up they were so sore. I spotted a rat.

It was chewing on some food so I went over to see if I could find something to eat for myself. It took whatever it was eating and ran away. There were big trash baskets all over in this park. But all I found was newspapers, bottles and junk. There was some gum stuck on a bench but I don't eat gum. I laid down to lick my sore paws and spotted a restaurant across from the park. I walked around the back of it to see if they had a dumpster.

I could smell food in them but couldn't reach the top and even if I could, I wouldn't be able to get anything since they had heavy covers on top. I continued searching for food as I walked. I passed a fast food place but they had heavy covers on their dumpsters too. I did find some scattered cold french fries and even though they were soggy I ate them but was still very hungry. I don't know what hurts more. My stomach from lack of food or my paws from walking.

The good Lord must be watching over me because I found a cold hamburger with only one bite taken out of it. Even though it was cold and the bun was hard I ate it slowly and enjoyed every bit of it. It filled up that big empty spot in my belly. It was getting darker and much colder and little white flakes of snow started to come down from the sky. I better find a safe place to stay for the night. My paws are so sore I don't think they can take another step. After a good nights rest I will probably feel a whole lot better and with the daylight it might feel a little warmer.

If I'm lucky I can find a barn or shed or a place under a porch until morning. I spotted an old condemned house that was deserted and figured it would have to do. At least I have a roof or should I say half a roof over my head. The windows are broken but with a couple of the walls still standing it should help to hold out some of the cold. I found a corner to lay down and cuddled to keep myself warm while I licked the blood off my sore paws. I seemed to fall fast asleep.

I heard a lot of noises, probably rats but I was to tired to even open my eyes. My body ached all over. I wondered if I did the right thing leaving the animal hospital where I had a warm place and food and nurses who cared about me. Boy I sure could use Doctor Hites for my bleeding paws. I wish I knew where Teezer lived, maybe I could live with her and that nice man and his other dog Lady. I wonder if that dog named Lady could be my sister Lady? I wish I knew where my other sisters lived maybe I could live with them.

After a good nights sleep I opened my eyes to see the bright sun shinning and decided I better start out again. It felt warmer with the sun and the wind died down and stopped snowing but I noticed that the black road was now covered with snow. As I walked on it my paws felt very cold but it helped to ease the pain in them. It started snowing again and was sticking all over my body which made me look like a white shepherd. I'm starting to blend in with the snow that all you can see are my black eyes.

I didn't know how long I've been walking on the roads or which way I was headed for. All I knew was that I had to keep on going. For all I knew I could be walking in circles and might end up back at the animal hospital. But nothing looked familiar. I saw cars and trucks, a school bus filled with kids, and people walking fast. There was a boy on his bike delivering newspapers and a Mailman putting mail in people's mailboxes. A Milkman delivering milk. Hey milk! That's what I need right now to survive.

I watched the Milkman as he went carrying a steel case holding bottles of milk in it, up some steps to a house and he left four bottles of milk on their porch near the front door. He went back to his truck and drove off. I looked around to check if the coast was clear. It was and I started up the steps on the porch and picked up one of the bottles filled with milk, and carried it carefully with my mouth down the steps, towards some bushes nearby.

I held the bottle between my sore paws and started to chew off the cap. With a little work I finally got it off. As I tilted the bottle on the ground the milk started to pour out. I lapped it up as fast as it came out. My little tongue never worked so fast. Oh boy! That sure filled me up and it tasted so good. I didn't like stealing the milk but I had no choice, I was starving. I hope God will forgive me. Days came and nights went and I walked miles and miles but I still didn't know where I would end up.

My paws hurt so bad I couldn't take one more step, I had to find a place that was safe for me to rest awhile. I saw a big gray barn that had the door slightly ajar and slid my tired body inside. There were horses and a lot of hay. The hay could keep me warm but I had to be careful that the horses didn't eat me up with it. I'll bet Teezer is nice and comfy and has plenty of food, and a playmate Lady to play with her.

I'll bet my other sisters are probably spoiled rotten by their owners. Right now I wish I had even just one of them. A owner, or a playmate, or a warm house or even a good meal. I'll have to forget about being hungry and then maybe the feeling will go away. All I want to do right now is rest, with that I fell asleep. I was even running in my sleep. I heard a dog whining in pain and it woke me up, to find out it was me whining.

I dreamt that nobody wanted me and the dog catcher had me and was ready to put me to sleep while he laughed, "ha, ha, ha, nobody wants you dog, now you'll be dead as a log, ha, ha, ha ". What a nightmare I must be getting punished for stealing the milk. I figured I better get moving before my nightmare comes true. I started out the barn door and I could smell something wonderful in the air. It was coming from the house across the barn. I couldn't leave until I found out what exactly smelled so darn good it made my mouth water.

A woman came out of the house and rang a triangular shaped bell of some kind. Men came running from the fields towards the house. The door was left open and I saw eight men sitting at a long table that was loaded with all kinds of different things to eat. There were flapjacks, sausages, eggs, bacon, homemade bread, butter, and jelly.

The Dog Nobody Wanted

The woman was pouring hot coffee into their cups. Boy that food sure looked just as good as it smelled.

Those men must of been very hungry because they wiped their plates clean with the bread. At a smaller table there were three children. One girl and two boys. They were also eating but had milk to drink not coffee. The men went back into the fields to do their chores. And when the children finished the girl stayed inside and helped the woman clean off the table and wiped the dishes while the woman washed them. The boys were sent out to play in the yard. One of the boys spotted me and came running towards me.

Look Mark a doggie, my doggie! No, Mike said it's my doggie! I saw it first. They both began to fight over me. The girl Maryann came running out of the house with the woman to see what the boys were fighting about. After hearing the boy's explanation of who's doggie it was, the woman said it's nobody's doggie. We have enough cats and dogs here already plus all the cows and pigs and horses and chickens. No more animals, we can't afford it.

But we can give this doggie a good meal and then send her on her way said the woman as she went into the house. Maryann picked me up and carried me into the house with Mark and Mike following and taking turns petting me. The nice woman cut up some of the sausages and bread and put it in a bowl and another bowl she poured some milk. I ate like there was no tomorrow. They all watched and laughed at the way I garbled my food and lapped my milk. My bowls were spotless. When I finished I let out a big burp and everyone giggled.

The woman must of been their mother because I heard them call her ma. She knew of some women Lana Buttons and Dorothy Bundy, who lived in Lockport and took in stray dogs and tried to find good homes for them. She gave them a phone call and explained the situation about finding the doggie and not being able to keep it. She told Lana that I didn't have any tags or a collar but was friendly and would make a good pet for someone.

Dorothy and Lana came over to take me right away. I was busy playing with Mark and Mike and Maryann. They walked over and picked me up and said, oh you poor thing, your nothing but skin and bone, and what happened to your ear? Don't you fret sweetie Lana and Dorothy will take good care of you. We'll fatten you up and fix those bloody paws too. And then we will get you in a home were you are loved.

They thanked the woman for calling them and put me in their van and we drove to their house. They didn't believe in dogs walking the streets so that they didn't get hurt and they were against putting dogs to sleep. So instead they found people that wanted and were good to animals or kept the dogs themselves.

When we got to their house there were a lot of dogs and they weren't in cages, they were running all over a big fenced in yard. There were some inside the house too. On couches, chairs even beds. All the dogs were friendly but very noisy. Lana ran an ad in the newspaper. Looking for someone to adopt homeless dogs with their phone number. They received a call the very next day from an elderly couple looking to adopt a dog. Dorothy and Lana drove me over to the couple's house for them to see me and decide if they wanted to keep me.

The couple said they would try me out because I was cute but if it didn't work out they would call Lana back to come and get me. I only lasted two days with them. Lana came to pick me up. They told her I jumped to much that they wanted a tamer dog. They just couldn't control my jumping all over them otherwise I was a good dog. So back I went to join the other dogs at Lana's and Dorothy's house. Two days later they got another call from an older man who was interested in a dog for companionship.

So they dropped me off to live with this man to see if we would get along. However he called Lana back the next day to come and get me that it didn't work out since I jumped on him to much and almost knocked him down. I just can't understand why these people hate my jumping on them. Don't they know how happy I am to have owners that love me, that's why I jump on them for joy. I like them.

Well anyway I'm back at Lana's and Dorothy's place with all the other homeless dogs just like me. Even though the ad was still in the newspaper, no one seemed to call to adopt any of us dogs. A week passed, two weeks, a month. And one day a woman called named Marge Seiders, who had lost her husband Robert who died in her arms of heart failure and two weeks later her dog Stormy died of old age and a broken heart.

She lived alone and wanted a dog bad. She said she loved dogs and had many 'til death do they part. And now she was very lonely and wanted a dog to give her something to live for. Marge always had dogs, when one died she always adopted another companion. She favored shepherds, because they were such a beautiful animal. German Shepherds, Belgium Shepherds and shepherd mix. All of a sudden I felt lucky. Maybe she will adopt me after all I'm a shepherd mix. I'll have to keep my paws crossed and hope and pray that she will take me home with her to be a loving companion to her.

Dorothy and Lana drove me all the way from Lockport to Burbank where the woman named Marge lived. I sure was nervous and wanted to make a good impression on her so she would keep me. By her driveway gates we stood. Marge on one side and me on the other. One look at this woman and I knew she was meant to be my owner for life. I was very lucky because she must have felt the same way since she decided to take me. It was like love at first sight when our eyes met.

Dorothy opened the gates and handed the leash over to my new owner. Lana gave Marge her usual speech, if things don't work out between you two please call us and we will come to take her back. They told Marge that I already was in a couple of homes and it didn't work out because I like to jump on people to much. Marge thanked them and said I don't think you'll be hearing from me to return her. They smiled and wished her luck and left saying good by to Stormy.

Now it was time for Stormy and me to get acquainted with each other. It felt like we were meant for one another. Marge introduced me to the big back yard to run around in and for potty calls. Then she took me into the house where I was to live with her. She showed me the kitchen and where my bowls for food and water were. Then I started to inspect the rest of the rooms. A living room with big windows that were from floor to ceiling that I could look out of.

I checked out the three bedrooms and a bathroom while Marge filled my dog dishes with dog food and water. She left me alone to eat while she went into the living room to watch the television. After I finished eating I decided to join her and jumped up on her lap and started licking her face to show her how grateful I was to be here. I then laid across her lap as she petted me and talked to me like I was a real person. I got very fidgety and she let me outside in the back yard for a potty call.

Boy did I have to go! I relieved myself as soon as my paws hit the grass. Marge praised me, saying good girl as she patted the top of my head. We both went back inside the house and she showed me a box filled with doggie toys. I grabbed a squeeker toy in a shape of a carrot and ran all over the house with it. It wore me out so I jumped back on Marge's lap and fell asleep as she continued to pet me.

Who would of dreamed that I could get so lucky with not only a owner that loved me but a box full of toys just for me. And most of all she doesn't mind that I jump on her either. Dorothy called to see how Marge and I were getting along. I heard Marge tell her it was the best thing that happened to her in a long time and said wild horses couldn't pull us apart, that she was keeping me forever. I was thrilled to hear that I now have a home and owner who loves me. I won't ever have to freeze outside or eat out of garbage cans anymore. I knew God would find a companion for me to love too.

How could things not work out between us? I had nobody and neither did Marge. Of course she does have her family but they are all married and have children of their own to worry about. Marge doesn't want to be dependent on any of them or be a pest. She said they have their own lives to live. I have Marge and she has me and we are dependent on each other for happiness and companionship. We did everything together eat, play, watch television, sleep and whatever.

I was like her shadow, wherever she was I was there too. Just like a bodyguard, I protected her while she watched over me. She put a small rug on her side of the bed for me to sleep on but I jumped up on the bed and slept next to her. Sometimes she would put her arm over me. Marge called her family to come over that she had a surprise for them. When they met me they complained that I jumped on them to much, shed my hair like crazy and my nails were to sharp.

But Marge didn't care she loved me and that's all that mattered. I was bigger then some of her grandchildren and I loved licking their faces although some of their mom's didn't appreciate it and would chase me away. The twin boys Dan and Steve like to play ball with me. Their brother Kevin, I think is afraid of me probably because I'm fast and wild. I don't mean to hurt them but I'm clumsy and there are times I knock them down, although I don't mean to. Chrissy just pets me but her brother Brian loves to wrestle with me and I love it.

Nicky likes to play tug of war with my rope pull toy with me on the other end of it. But little Marissa runs when she sees me coming towards her. I guess I scare her when I jump on her. We are both about the same size except when I jump, I'm bigger then her. I love it when the grown ups rough house with me. The rougher they get the more I like it. I am pretty strong.

I like being babied like when Marge brushes me. It feels so good I wish she would never stop. She sure does get a lot of my hair on that brush. If it keeps up I will be a bald dog. I guess shepherds shed a lot. I hate bath time. Marge laughs that I look like a drowned rat when I'm all wet but I get even with her when I shake myself dry and get her soaking wet. It looks like she got the bath not me.

Marge takes good care of me. I got all my shots and get regular check ups. She gives me a vitamin daily and a heartworm pill once a month. Around my neck I wear a collar that has a tag with my name and address and phone number to call if I ever got lost. There is another tag for my license and one for rabies and a doggie angel medal to protect me. I got the medal from Iris Martinsen, a friend of Marge's who lives in Indiana. I get all kinds of treats and toys from everyone in the family on holidays.

Marge brags about me to everyone and even signs all her cards and letters Marge and Stormy too. She enjoys taking lots of pictures of me and shows them off to everyone.

Marge couldn't figure out why no one wanted me because to her I was a great companion except for my jumping but then no one is perfect. She said it was a shame that her husband was dead because Robert would of liked me too. He loved dogs and was very attached to their dog, who died two weeks after Robert died from a stroke. But Marge said he really died from a broken heart. Now her husband has his dog in heaven with him and Marge has me forever.

I enjoy every minute we share together but I still see sadness in Marge's eyes. I heard her say there was something missing in her life. She could talk to me and I understood but I can't hold a conversation with her. She would kiss me and I would lick her but it wasn't the same as a man would kiss her. I could put my paw on her shoulder but it wasn't the same as when a man would wrap his arms around her.

Was I the reason she didn't find a man because of my jumping? One day she turned to me with tears in her eyes and said, you know what Stormy, I found you through an ad in the newspaper and it has worked out great for us. I think I will try to find a nice gentleman the same way. What have I got to lose? The newspaper carried columns where men are seeking the company of a woman and females are looking for male companionship. Each ad gave some information about what they wanted and their likes and dislikes. It described a little about themselves and their interests. Some wanted a woman to get married while others were just looking for companionship. Their hobbies, age…what the heck, what have I got to lose? If I didn't like talking to them I didn't have to go out with them. I read a few and found one that seemed interesting so I called. The first one was a crack pot and I told him I wouldn't waste my time on him. He was just out for one thing and I wasn't interested. I'm not out for a marriage just someone to go to a movie or have dinner with, heck I'll even cook the meal. I just wanted someone to talk to that would understand how I felt, lonely.

I dialed another to find he had a one track mind and was looking for a one night stand, good by baby. Another call was a misfit too. Gee aren't there any descent men out there just looking for companionship? I tried one more call but he sounded drunk and I hung up. I got very disgusted and quit calling but I still kept reading the ads everyday.

Then one day there was this ad that seemed to interest me. This male liked the same things I did and he loved dogs. So I taught I have nothing to lose and dialed his number. There was no answer so I left my name and number on his answering machine to call me. When he called me, he was very soft spoken. I told him a little about myself and he in return told me about himself. We talked about our likes and dislikes. He was very easy to talk to and I was at ease talking to him.

I told him about my dog Stormy and he laughed. We both had a lot in common. We talked for almost two hours and he said he had to go to work that he worked nights but would call again and we could continue our conversation. I said that would be nice and told him good by and not to work to hard and hung up. I felt that he just brushed me off nicely because it was to far for him to travel to see me since he lived in Lynwood and I lived in Burbank.

I turned off the television, let Stormy out for the night and we both turned in for the night. Stormy on one side of the bed and me on the other. I guess from talking so much I wore myself out and fell asleep right away. The next morning Stormy woke me up licking my face. It was time for her potty call. I let her out and put on the pot for coffee. Filled up her dishes with fresh water and food and made some toast for myself.

The Dog Nobody Wanted

I gave Stormy her vitamin and took mine as well, turned on the television to find out the weather and ate my toast with the coffee. I cleaned up the house and washed some clothes. Then got dressed and went outside to sprinkle the lawn and flowers. Stormy had fun chasing the birds and squirrels. I went behind the garage to sprinkle my vegetable garden. Everything was starting to sprout. It was such a beautiful day. I then gave Stormy a good brushing which she really enjoyed. We played ball for awhile then came inside.

I was surprised when the phone rang and it was that nice man again. Hi, I said, I'm sorry but I don't even know your name. He told me it was Robert Metz. We continued our conversation from where we left off. He lived in a mobile home with his two dogs, Teezer a Shih-Tzu and an Australian Shepherd named Lady. He was divorced and one year and four months older then me. He was of German descent, went to a catholic church but was of no religion.

We both enjoyed going to estate and garage sales, movies, casinos, tours, long drives by the lake, walking, but he also ran a lot and joined the health club. Our taste in music was the same country, rock and roll, the oldies, polkas and the blues. I loved dancing but he said he had. two left feet and wasn't good at dancing. He had four kids. Bobby, Michael, and Dan and a daughter Sherri. He had grand kids. Neither one of us smoked although we did long time ago.

We enjoyed a drink occasionally. He was looking for a woman that he could trust, and wanted companionship not a marriage. This was great because that's exactly what I was looking for too. He said okay now you tell me about yourself. I told Robert I was Catholic and a widow for a year. I lived with my best friend Stormy. I loved to bake and cook. Was crazy about dogs. I said I had a perfect marriage with the best husband anyone could have and when he died part of me went with him, two weeks later my dog died too.

I told him I had four children, all were married except for MaryAnn who died and was in heaven. My son Michael was married to Joann and lived in Tinley Park with two children. My grand daughter Christina and grandson Brian. My oldest daughter Marcia was married to John and lived in Crestwood with my twin grandsons Steven and Daniel who are twins and Kevin. And my baby Maria Elena who was married to Ronald and had two children, my grandson Nicholas and grand daughter Marissa in Berwyn.

They all have dogs too. We are a dog loving family. I mentioned that I have two sisters. Eva who was a widow now and Rosemarie who was married to Arthur. Bob said he hated to cut me short but he has to take his dog out and get ready for work since he worked the night shift, but promised to call me again that he really enjoys talking to me.

I let Stormy out for the night and turned on the television when the phone rang. It was Robert calling me back. He said work was slow so he had time to talk. He was a diesel mechanic at Pals Cartage on the midnight shift. He asked if we could meet that he enjoyed talking to me. We set a time, 2:00 tomorrow in the daytime since he worked nights. I gave him my address and he asked if I would like to take a walk along Lake Michigan where we could talk and get acquainted. I agreed. He said fine I'll see you then. He has to meet Stormy and if she doesn't like him I won't go out with him. Dogs can tell a lot about people and I trust her judgement.

At 2:00 the next day the doorbell rang. Well he was punctual. I was a little nervous to open the door but as long as Stormy was at my side I felt safe. There stood this 5' 10" gentleman, with blondish light brown hair, hazel eyes, dressed neatly, clean shaven and gosh he smelled oh so good. My heart started doing flip flops.

I invited Robert in and he sat down on the couch in the living room and Stormy was all over him like a pest. I offered to put her away but he insisted that I leave her be. He didn't mind one bit that she was jumping on him and played with her as we talked. Stormy was really over acting, she was being a brat. We decided to go for a ride in his pickup to lake Michigan and walk along the shoreline and talk without Stormy.

He opened the truck door for me as I got in. I think we both were a little nervous. He drove nice not like a maniac. We talked on the way there and when we arrived at the lake Robert helped me out of the truck and held my hand as we walked all around the shoreline. The conversation never stopped, it was as if we knew each other for a long time. He was very easy to talk to. His hands were nice and warm and strong just like my husbands were. On the way back home I invited him back to my house.

We ate homemade cake and drank coffee while we looked at some photo albums filled with memories.

The Dog Nobody Wanted

There were pictures of trips, my children, my grandkids, our dogs, my sisters, parents, vacations, weddings, baptism's, grand parents and friends. I couldn't believe Stormy. She just wouldn't leave Robert alone. When we went into the living room to sit on the couch, Stormy parked her butt right between the both of us and wanted all of his attention. Robert never chased her away but enough is enough. I put her in the kitchen for awhile so we could talk in peace.

After that day we started to see each other everyday and he called me every night from work to talk. We figured now was a good time for Robert to introduce his dogs Lady and Teezer to Stormy to see if they would get along as well as we did. I must admit I was afraid that if they didn't get along it was so long Robert it's been good to know you. I was worried since Stormy liked to rough house that maybe she would hurt Robert's dogs unintentionally.

But when Stormy met Lady and Teezer it was like she knew them and acted like a mama would to her children. They went up to each other rubbing noses and wagging their tails. Then all of them started chasing one another around the yard. They got along beautifully. Stormy was very gentle towards them. They played so hard and when they tired out all three dogs seem to snuggle together and fell fast asleep. What a pretty sight to see. It was as if we were all one family. They got along just as well as Robert and I did. It was like Stormy grew up over night. What a sight for sore eyes, it was beautiful.

We took the three dogs with us for long rides in the truck. Teezer on my lap and Stormy and Lady in the back seat. We all enjoyed the long walks in the forest preserves. When we ate, they ate. They shared their toys with one another. And Robert and I spent equal time with each dog so no one would be jealous. On Halloween we dressed them up. Stormy was a devil with red horns on her head and a red cape and long red tail which fit her because she was full of the devil at times.

Little Teezer was dressed as an angel with a halo on her head and wings on her back. And Lady was dressed like a baby with a bonnet on her head and a big bib on her chest and a pacifier that was real big and hung from her neck. The grandkids got a kick out of them, even the neighbors taught they looked cute and gave them doggie treats for trick or treat.

We sure were having a lot of fun, all five of us. At Christmas time they got gifts just like we did except it wasn't clothes or jewelry or perfume. They got doggie treats like pig ears and cow hooves with doggie cookies and squeaky dog toys. All my children bought them gifts too. They were all spoiled rotten but then they deserved to be since they were making us happy by just being with us everyday. They bought laughter back into the house and in our lives.

One day when Robert was over he suggested that as long as we got along so well and the dogs did too that we should become one big happy family. What do you think about becoming Mrs. Metz, Marge? I taught he was kidding until he pulled out a ring. I didn't even hesitate to answer him with a yes but I'll have to ask Stormy to see how she feels about it.

I walked over where Stormy was laying with Teezer and Lady and asked her, Stormy, how would you like it if we adopted Robert and Teezer and Lady? I felt like she knew what I was saying because she started licking my face and wagging her tail and soon Lady and Teezer were doing the same. I looked at Robert and said I guess it's final since everyone agrees we should all be one big happy family with a mama, a papa and three doggies.

Little did we know that Teezer, Lady and Stormy were sisters that got separated shortly after they were born. The happiness that I sought had filled my heart when we were married and the ring was placed on my left hand till death do us part. I will never forget my husband Robert Seiders, he will always have a place in my heart because I loved him so much. But life must go on and I know he is happy for me now. I never believed I could find happiness but here it is. Maybe Robert helped us to get together. Whatever it was I'm glad we found. each other and married.

I'm just lucky he liked dogs because I could never get rid of Stormy, she was part of me. We all honeymooned in Monticello, Indiana. Robert and I and the rest of our family, Stormy, Teezer and Lady. We are one big happy family. Stormy took over and acts like their mother and protector. She guards them every minute. Teezer and Lady won't even go outside without their pal Stormy.

They are inseparable and very happy now that we are all together. It's like a dream come true. It's a one in a million chance of finding one another but we all did it with the help of God. One for all and all for one. Our luck has changed for the better. No more sad or bad times, and if there is I know we can handle it together.

The dog nobody wanted has finally found true happiness, a family that loves her, a nice warm home filled with love, caring owners, and two of her lost sisters are back with her again. What more could a dog want? She is so happy that when the other dogs are sleeping and she is near them, that bent ear leans towards them as if to say, those are my sisters as her tail wags happily. I feel that I don't own Stormy, she owns me. It's the same as being married to our dogs when you take your vows 'til death do us part. Just as many books have a happy ending so does this one. And they all lived happily ever after with *THE DOG NOBODY WANTED.*

THE END